World War II Battle of Britain

A History From Beginning to End

Table of Contents

Introduction

When Winston Churchill became prime minister of Great Britain on May 10, 1940, he was embarking upon a perilous time in his political career and in his nation's history. Germany had already conquered Poland, Norway, and Denmark and was on its way to overpowering Belgium, Luxembourg, the Netherlands, and France. Only the British remained as an obstacle to Hitler's goal of dominating Europe, and the Fuhrer was assured that no one could stand in his way.

Hermann Goering had promised that his Luftwaffe would bring England to submission by bombing the nation relentlessly, setting the buildings on fire and teaching the English that they were foolish to think that they could stand against the might of the Third Reich. The English public, Goering promised, would be terrified and would force its government to submit to whatever terms the Germans offered in exchange for peace and an end to the bombing. That was how the Germans expected the story to unfold.

But the British were not interested in peace on German terms. Well aware that, with France having surrendered to Germany and the United States intent on remaining neutral in what they regarded as a European conflict, the British stood alone, the people took courage from Churchill's words, "We shall never surrender."

The Germans would test that boast as their planes crossed the English Channel to pound the British with bombs. Taking refuge in air raid shelters became a way of life for the beleaguered civilians, and on one night, the London Underground provided protection for more than 170,000 people. The toll on human life was punishing; between July 1940 and May 1941 when the Battle of Britain officially ended, more than 40,000 civilians had lost their lives. The streets of London were crowded with the rubble from the buildings that had been damaged in the bombing raids. How could they endure such devastation?

But a surprising thing happened on the way to the German domination of the air. The Royal Air Force, alerted by radar when the planes were approaching, flew up into the sky to meet the enemy and Goering's boast was proven to be hollow. "Never in the field of human conflict," Churchill said, "has so much been owed by so many to so few."

The Germans were convinced that the RAF was at the end of its ability to meet the Luftwaffe in battle, but somehow, the pilots continued to do so. The Battle of Britain, the first military engagement fought entirely between enemy air forces, would be the first defeat that the Germans would suffer.

But the Battle of Britain was more than a military encounter. It was a test of the human will. Before the Germans began their bombing campaign, many English children were sent from London for their own safety. Some were sent to the countryside, where the threat of bombing was less. Some were even sent abroad, to Canada and the United States. But Queen Elizabeth of England set the tone when, after some people said that she and King George VI should go to Canada to be safe, answered that "The children will not leave unless I do. I shall not leave unless their father does, and the King will not leave the country in any circumstances whatever."

It was that spirit that demonstrated the resolve of the British people. They would not give in. As bombs rained down from the sky during the day and the night, as fires blazed in the streets and homes exploded and landmarks were struck, as people crowded the shelters and the Underground seeking refuge, they did not surrender. Had the people been less resilient, perhaps the government would have been forced to accept Hitler's terms and seek peace at any price.

Instead, the people of Great Britain accepted the fact that freedom came with a price tag. Churchill had not minimized the threats that they faced, nor had he sugar-coated the task that lay before them. But civilization was worth saving, and if the Nazis were allowed to win, they would enter a new Dark Age. Of this, Churchill was certain, and he did not mince words as he made the case for Great Britain to rise to the occasion. Therefore, Churchill, who was a historian as much as he was a politician, summoned his people to accept their destiny. "Let us therefore brace ourselves to our duties, and so bear ourselves that, if the British Empire and its Commonwealth last for a thousand years, men will say, 'This was their finest hour.'"

Chapter One

Sitzkrieg, the Sitting War

"My personal view is that the only thing achieved was largely to supply the continent's requirements of toilet paper for the five long years of the war."

—Arthur "Bomber" Harris

The British could have been forgiven for believing that, despite the German invasion of Poland beginning at 4:45 am on September 1, 1939, and Prime Minister Chamberlain's declaration of war on September 3, nothing much was going to happen. The declaration of war against Germany was followed by air raid sirens, indicating that attack was imminent, but the warnings proved to be a mistake. Later, that would not be the case, but in 1939, war seemed unreal. Nonetheless, the British people prepared for battle, sending their children to the country so that they would be safe from the expected Luftwaffe bombing.

The people of Poland were relieved at the declaration of war that followed the German invasion of their country, convinced that they would be rescued from the Nazi invaders. But as the Germans drove further from the west, soon to be followed by the Soviet invasion from the east, the Polish people realized that the Allied declaration of war was an arsenal of words only. Approximately three million Polish citizens would be sent to Germany to work as slaves; the Germans regarded Slavs as racially inferior and intended to eradicate the population. The country of Poland would provide Lebensraum or "living space" for the Germans so that they could expand their borders. Occupied Poland became the site of the deadly concentration and extermination camps run by the Nazis; names such as Auschwitz, Birkenau, Treblinka, and Sobibor became synonymous with death as the Nazis pursued their annihilation of Jews and others.

Poland was not a magnet for Allied defense, despite the British promise to defend the nation. But France was, and everyone knew that France was a German target. The Germans had never forgiven the French for the humiliating terms that had been inflicted on Germany at the end of World War I. The two countries, longstanding adversaries, viewed one another as natural foes. Once again, they would go to war.

So it was that the British Expeditionary Force began to arrive in France on September 4, but the build-up of troops provided no aid to the Poles. On September 12, 1939, the British and French Supreme War Council met to decide that the Allies would end their offensive operations in order to fight a defensive war. The British sent four divisions consisting of 158,000 men with 25,000 vehicles; it was a small force to mount against the Nazis, but the French were confident that their well-defended Maginot Line along the border between France and Germany would keep Hitler's armies from invading.

The map of Europe was swiftly changing as the Soviet Union, performing as agreed in the Non-Aggression Pact it had signed with Germany, occupied Estonia, Latvia, and Lithuania and defeated Finland. But as 1939 came to an end, war seemed to be something that was happening to other countries, not to the English.

For eight months, mounting an attack against the German aggressors seemed to be the farthest thing from anyone's mind. Meanwhile, the British and their French allies began planning for operations that were intended to hamper the accelerating conflict. The Allies opened a front up in the Balkans in their effort to shut off the supply of oil to the Soviet Union. They also sought to thwart the Nazis from obtaining iron ore from Norway.

The Germans, however, were not idle after their invasion of Poland. German U-boats sank more than 100 merchant vessels en route to Britain during the first four months of the war. The Battle of the Atlantic got underway shortly after the declaration of war. Great Britain had long believed that it owned the seas, but the German U-boats were showing signs of challenging that reputation as they sank the HMS *Royal Oak* in October.

Hitler had told his U-boat commanders not to attack passenger liners unless they were obviously traveling as part of a convoy. Claiming to believe that the *Athenia*, a ship bound for Canada, was a naval vessel, the Germans attacked. The attack cost 112 people their lives; the Germans insisted that the poor light had made it difficult to discern the nature of the ship. Besides, the commander said, British intelligence had placed a bomb aboard the ship.

The British were engaged in bombing missions over Germany, but the results were hardly going to strike fear in the hearts of the people who had confidence in the power of their Luftwaffe. The British planes dropped millions of leaflets from the skies over Germany, and while the raids demonstrated that the air was not impregnable, their purpose was to convince the Germans that their regime was evil. On the night of September 3, the British dropped the equivalent of 13 tons of paper when it sent "Note to the German People."

British General Spears derisively referred to the bombing as a "confetti war" one which would be useless against what he termed a ruthless enemy. But there seemed to be a gentlemen's agreement at work among the British hierarchy which held that rules prohibited certain targets from being struck. At the suggestion that the Black Forest ought to be bombed because the Germans were so very fond of their trees, Sir Kingsley Wood, the Secretary of State for Air, was aghast. The Black Forest could not be bombed, he explained; it was private property.

Although there seemed to be no clear-cut definition of what constituted a war, the home front was in preparation. Blackouts were underway. No lighting of any description was permitted within 12 miles of the island's southeastern coast. But faced with the issue of traffic accidents harming pedestrians, Westminster allowed low-density streetlights beginning in December 1939.

More effort was concentrated on preparing the people of Britain for the attack that the government knew was inevitable. In order to keep the Luftwaffe at bay, barrage balloons—which would force the German Air Force to fly higher, thereby reducing their accuracy—were deployed. Thirty-eight million gas masks were distributed; people who were going to the movies were not admitted if they did not bring their gas mask with them. The poisonous snakes in the London Zoo were euthanized to avoid any risk to civilians in case they escaped during a bombing raid. A total of 400 million sandbags were stacked around the city's buildings.

In January 1940, Allied intelligence discovered that the Germans were planning to attack the Low Countries soon. When the Allies made their move to begin preparations to defend Belgium, the Germans altered course, a decision which would have fateful consequences for the French while galvanizing the Germans.

But nothing was happening in England. People began to relax and carry on with the lives they had lived before war was declared. Why carry a gas mask everywhere when there was no indication that it would be needed?

Then, suddenly, the calm was replaced by action. When the Germans invaded Denmark and Norway on April 9, 1940, Allied troops responded, but their efforts were unimpressive. Beginning on April 14, they began landing in Norway, but it seemed that there was no stopping the German advance. By the end of April, the Germans had a firm grip on southern Norway. Then, when the Germans invaded France, the Allies left Norway. On June 9, the Norwegian military surrendered.

Chapter Two

The Phoney War Ends

"Britain and France had to choose between war and dishonor. They chose dishonor. They will have war."

—Winston Churchill

For Germany, the map of Europe was relevant in terms of what the Germans lacked and what its military had to do in order to obtain what was needed. Because Germany imported ten million tons of iron ore from Sweden, a port was needed that did not freeze in the winter months. That port, Narvik, was in northern Norway. Furthermore, control of the Norwegian coastline would give Germany easy passage through the North Sea to the Atlantic Ocean. Great Britain's military scoffed at the notion that the Germans would be able to successfully invade Norway, and the Norwegians trusted that the British Navy would assist if the Germans did attempt an invasion.

On March 1, 1940, Hitler issued an order for the invasion of Denmark and Norway. The Phoney War, which had begun on September 3, was about to come to an end. On April 7, 1940, an attack by British bombers against German warships proved to be unsuccessful, but it did point out that Germany's vessels were at risk from attack. A violent storm and poor conditions, however, made it possible for the Germans to conceal their efforts at landing troops in northern Norway without being impeded by the British. The Norwegians lacked the resources to defend against attack; two ships assigned to defend the coast sank, with only 8 men out of the 182-man crew surviving.

The surprise attack by the Germans was so effective that the local commander at the port of Narvik thought the ships were from the British Navy coming to help. Norway intended to defend the port but decided to surrender when the German response warned that defense would lead to an unnecessary loss of life. That surrender was the beginning of defeat as other cities in Norway surrendered. Denmark gave way quickly as King Christian X ordered an end to resistance against the Germans.

The Germans were not going to stop with Norway. The prize was France, but first, there was the Netherlands. Germany believed that their success was assured if they could frighten the Dutch into surrendering. In order to do that, they launched the terror of the blitzkrieg, and their plan worked; the Dutch surrendered in six days.

The Scandinavian countries were not Hitler's ultimate target, but they were strategically significant. Occupying Denmark would provide Germany with naval bases, and it would protect the iron-ore shipments from Sweden that Germany needed. The German explanation for its invasion of the two countries was sanitized to make the claim that Germany was protecting Denmark and Norway against what it described as the aggression of the Allied powers.

Belgium was next. Belgian neutrality was ignored, as it had been in the First World War. The Germans sent their divisions, paratroopers, and air gliders to conquer Belgium. The Belgians did not give up without a fight, but after 18 days, the military surrendered. King Leopold III surrendered on May 28 although his failure to consult his government on the matter was criticized. Countries that formerly had been free now flew the swastika; they were occupied by the Germans, who were on their way to France.

The Allies had cause to be confident about their superiority over the Germans. For one thing, they were not Poland or the Scandinavian countries or the Low Countries; they had military advantages that the others lacked. Not only did they have more tanks, but their tanks were better. They were enthusiastic about their armored warfare advantages and felt that they had the ground forces to stun the Germans into defeat. An army that still remembered the numbing inertia of World War I's trench warfare was eager to show its might through rapid movement.

The Germans, with their air superiority, had the advantage in the skies. The Allied planes were not offering support to the ground troops; their role was to provide aerial reconnaissance and defense. Also, they lacked the German ground-to-air communication which made a synchronized attack much more efficient.

The Germans remembered trench warfare, too. The Germans knew that it was not just imperative to win the fighting; it was necessary to demoralize the enemy as well.

Germany's General Erich von Manstein had a plan that would, he assured Hitler, catch the Allies off guard and allow the German Army to blitzkrieg its way to a victory that would devastate the French. Instead of sending its main offensive through the Low Countries, the Germans should advance further south through the Ardennes forest and go directly into France, avoiding the expected challenge at the Maginot Line.

The Allies, who believed that the terrain of the Ardennes would be too difficult as a means of transport for the troops, would be duped into believing that the Low Countries were the focus of the advance because Germany's Army Group B would invade Belgium as expected, while Army Group A's Panzers would cut off the entire British army and much of the French army as well. They would race to the coast with seven armored divisions. The risks were considerable and included an exposed flank with no infantry support behind them. Lose now, and the war was over.

As the German forces emerged from the Ardennes and headed toward the coast of the English Channel, having outflanked the Maginot Line upon which the Allies had based their confidence, the British Expeditionary Force was in danger of being surrounded. Germany knew how to capitalize on massed tank formations; the Poles had not known how to counter it, and apparently the Allies didn't know either.

But the Allies did not believe that movement had been seen in the Ardennes. They were convinced that their forces were holding the Germans along the northern front in Belgium and the Netherlands and that the movement around the Ardennes was only a diversionary tactic. The failure to respond cost them. Within three days, the German armored units had made their way through the rough terrain of the Ardennes and crossed the river Meuse. Allied plans to gradually retreat to the Meuse were now pointless.

Germany's Army Group A reached the mouth of the river Somme on the English Channel by May 20, trapping the main forces of Great Britain and France. In order to survive, the British began to fall back and head to Dunkirk. Complete defeat seemed certain. Then, on May 24, Hitler was persuaded that the Germans needed to give the tanks a rest so that they could destroy the French Army. Luftwaffe commander Hermann Goering was confident that his air force would be able to destroy the British army gathering at Dunkirk.

Given a brief respite from the German decision to rest, the British prepared for the evacuation and, although no one realized it at the time, the preservation of the British military. On May 24, the German advance halted. On May 27, it began anew. While the Luftwaffe attacked from the skies, the British evacuation, aided by more than 800 "little ships" that had responded to their nation's call to rescue more than 300,000 trapped soldiers, got underway. As the German planes flew overhead, the lines of soldiers waiting to board ships had to hurry to the dunes to avoid being hit.

Winston Churchill, Great Britain's new prime minister, applauded his nation's feat but warned the people that wars were not won by evacuations. He knew that, with the fall of France, the British will would be sorely tested as the British stood alone against the victorious Germans who had subjugated the nations of Europe.

Chapter Three

Battle for the Skies

"What General Weygand called the Battle of France is over. I expect that the Battle of Britain is about to begin. The whole fury and might of the enemy must very soon be turned on us now. Hitler knows that he will have to break us in this island or lose the war. If we can stand up to him, all Europe may be free . . . But if we fail, then the whole world, including the United States, including all that we have known and cared for, will sink into the abyss of a new Dark Age."

—Winston Churchill

On May 15, the French prime minister telephoned Winston Churchill to tell him that the French had been beaten by the Germans. The German blitzkrieg had charged through Belgium and the Netherlands, crossed the Meuse River, and attacked the French army at Sedan on the northern end of the Maginot Line, the 280-mile long stretch of fortifications which was designed to protect the French from the Germans.

The Maginot Line proved to be no match for the German tanks and planes. On June 14, the Germans marched into Paris, and the city was divided into two zones, one under the control of the Germans and the other under the control of former World War I hero Marshal Philippe Petain, now the leader of the Vichy Government. But the distinction was superfluous; Germany ruled France.

Churchill had become prime minister on May 10, the day that the Nazis mounted their attack against France, Belgium, Luxembourg, and the Netherlands. But Churchill was not cowed by the less-than-encouraging alignment of the fates which would render Great Britain as the only declared opponent still standing after the Germans summer of martial success. Even though the Germans dispatched the free nations of Europe with seeming ease, Churchill felt a sense of relief. Later, he would write, "At last I had authority to give directions over the whole scene. I felt as if I were walking with destiny, and that all my past life had been but a preparation for this hour and this trial."

As the dominant power in Europe, Germany was confident that any terms it offered to the British would be accepted with relief. Why, Hitler wondered, would the British bother to remain at war with the victorious Germans who had clearly proven their ability to crush their enemies? Some in the British government agreed with this view and would have preferred a settlement with Germany rather than a prolonged war that could leave Great Britain in the same state as the rest of Europe. But Chamberlain had refused a settlement, and Churchill felt the same way.

Perhaps the British knew better than to trust Hitler. Three days before he offered terms of peace to the British,

Hitler's directive for Operation Sea Lion had already been issued. The invasion of southern England was scheduled for autumn, after the Luftwaffe had demolished the RAF. Germany's plan was to destroy the Royal Air Force and, once air superiority was achieved, pressure the British to accept peace terms. Directive No. 16, *On preparations for a landing operation against England*, Hitler's timeline for Operation Sea Lion, was to be ready by the middle of August unless Great Britain came to the negotiating table. Directive No. 17, *For the conduct of air and sea warfare against England* intended to see the Luftwaffe gain air superiority over southern England so that the invasion could proceed as a credible threat.

Numerically, the Luftwaffe had the advantage over the RAF, with 1,223 fighters, 1,482 bombers, and 327 dive bombers, compared to less than 2,000 total aircraft on the part of the Royal Air Force. The British needed help in order to mount a defense. Just as the government had done when it called upon the people of Britain to rescue the soldiers stranded at Dunkirk, it sent out another plea, this time for all available aluminum. The Ministry of Aircraft Production promised, "We will turn your pots and pans into Spitfires and Hurricanes."

The British also had another means of defense which, while it could not prevent the Germans from bombing Britain, could at least prevent it from doing so without being noticed. The country had a very effective radar system that would be capable of detecting the incoming German aircraft as they flew over the English Channel. Radio Direction Finding, or radar, was developed in the

1930s and the British wasted no time in constructing a ring of "Chain Home" radar stations along the coastline. Although primitive, the radar system could identify the locations of the Luftwaffe aircraft, send up fighters to intercept them, and prevent the Germans from surprising the British when they came raiding.

The RAF also benefitted from the effectiveness of their aircraft. The British Spitfire, because it could turn tighter, could more effectively elude its pursuers. The Hurricanes could carry 40mm cannon. In comparison, the limited flight radius of the German single-engine fighters and the inadequate bomb-load capacity of the German bombers would benefit the RAF.

Although the Germans began to attack shipping along the English coast at the beginning of July, the recognized start of the Battle of Britain, regarded as the first significant military campaign to be entirely conducted by enemy air forces, was July 10, 1940. That morning, British radar picked up the signal that German reconnaissance planes were in search of convoys to attack. The Battle of Britain officially began as 120 German aircraft attacked a British shipping convoy in the English Channel. Dockyard installations in south Wales were struck by 70 German bombers. The purpose was to attack the shipping lanes so that England would not receive the material and supplies it needed, as well as to entice RAF fighters to come forth so that they would be drawn into engagement with the Luftwaffe's fighter escorts.

By afternoon, radar indicated that another significant force of German aircraft had appeared. Half a dozen

Hurricanes were patrolling a convoy of vessels; in the ensuing battle, three Hurricanes and four Luftwaffe plans were lost, and one coastal ship sank. In that first day of fighting, the RAF flew 609 sorties; the RAF would have to continue to fly a large number of sorties if they hoped to be able to intercept the Luftwaffe as it came raiding. In order to be ready for the next sortie, the planes had to be re-armed and refueled as soon as they returned from battle.

The Luftwaffe admittedly possessed great advantages, and their intelligence should have been one of them. As far back as the summer of 1939, the German *Graf Zeppelin*, which flew along the British coastline listening in on RAF transmissions, learned that the pilots were controlled from facilities on the ground. They knew that the British had a radar system. But they did not know about the top-secret Dowding system which was linked with fighter control. And because they assumed that the ground control procedures were rigid, they miscalculated the strength of the RAF Fighter Command. When the Luftwaffe intelligence encountered information which did not match their own perceptions, they ignored it. The Germans based their operational plans on a report that claimed that RAF pilots were tied to their home bases. With such constraints, the Germans reasoned, the RAF would be easy pickings.

Day after day, as the German aircraft flew across the Channel in their efforts to lure the British pilots into battle, the RAF responded. On August 18, the Luftwaffe flew 850 sorties; the RAF responded with 927 sorties. The RAF lost 68 aircraft; the Luftwaffe 69.

Pilot officer John Beard, a member of a squadron of Hurricanes based near London, recalled an encounter with the Germans. As he was waiting for his plane to be rearmed and refueled, he learned that Germans were heading up from the Thames toward London. The pilots raced to their planes, leveled off at 15,000 feet and waited. As he switched on his reflector sight, flicked the gun button catch from "Safe" to "Fire," and lowered his seat until the reflector light was dark red in front of his eyes, he heard the tactical orders being issued from the squadron leader.

Steadying the fighter, just as he would have steadied a rifle before firing, Beard dove onto the tail of a line of Heinkels. The Heinkel he had chosen appeared in the red dot. Beard pressed the button and fired upon the Heinkel with a pair of two-second bursts. Flames shot out along the fuselage, and the Heinkel went spinning as pieces of the plane flew off. This was the life of an RAF pilot during the Battle of Britain.

Between July and September of 1940, the Luftwaffe targeted its raids upon the shipping, warehouses, and ports in order to do damage to the ability of the British to provide food for the civilians. But destroying the RAF was always a priority, and on August 13, the Germans began a determined effort to attack the RAF airfields.

The two-month campaign resulted in a loss of 1,733 aircraft by the Germans, while the RAF lost 915. The RAF was making its mark as a force to be reckoned with. In a speech to the House of Commons on August 20, Churchill commemorated the valor of the Royal Air Force in stirring words. "Never in the field of human conflict has so much been owed by so many to so few."

Chapter Four

The Home Front

"It was terrible last night. We were up for nine hours and the sky was lit by the most lurid glow from the tremendous fires in London. I watched the flames and the planes and the guns and I thought of you and had a terrible feeling that you were in danger. Please, my darling, do not get hurt. Please keep alive for me to come back to you, to love you and look after you and see my beautiful baby again. I am now living without sleep and I suppose you are too, and that is much worse. A peaceful night now seems too remote to be considered."

—Lieutenant John Belsey

Winston Churchill had declared in his speech to the House of Commons on June 4, 1940, "We shall never surrender," and he meant it, although others in Great Britain would have been amenable to accepting some kind of terms from Germany. Hitler reasoned that an all-out bombing attack on the British public would serve multiple purposes; he expected that relentless bombing would weaken the resolve of the British people so that they would pressure the British government into accepting Hitler's terms. The bombing would also destroy the RAF, leaving Great Britain without air defenses and making the Luftwaffe the master of the skies.

The new twist to the war would turn British civilians into domestic frontline forces. Citizens accepted their new roles as defenders of their homeland, taking positions in local organizations designed to protect their communities in the likelihood of attack. Children were evacuated to the country so that they would be safe; some were even evacuated out of the country to Canada, Australia, and the United States. When children were evacuated, they took with them their gas masks, books, clothes, a few small toys, their ration books, and money. Separation was hard on families, but the British population knew that Hitler would spare no effort to bring their nation to its knees. Facing such a scenario, they wanted their children to be safe, and that meant leaving London and, sometimes, Great Britain.

British civilians did have to adjust to some privations; there was food rationing just like in Germany, where most of the food supply was under the control of the German government. In addition to food, gasoline, clothing, and leather were also rationed. As many British people already had or planted gardens, they were able to increase their food supply, particularly in the surrounding countryside, where they had more space for their gardens and more access to products that weren't rationed. Even food had a military use, as fat was conserved to be used for the production of nitroglycerin.

Preparation for a bombing attack on civilians had actually begun earlier, before the war officially got underway. The world knew that civilians in China and Spain had endured air raids and recognized this as a new and terrible facet of modern war. Aerial warfare had been a feature of World War I, but the advance of technology had turned the skies into a field of battle that would be just as significant as those fought on land. The government devised several different air raid shelters to protect its citizens from the onslaught of terror from the skies that everyone knew was on its way.

Anderson Shelters, named after the Home Secretary Sir John Anderson, were designed to be used in gardens. They were buried halfway into the ground with soil on top to provide protection from the fragments of shells and bomb splinters. Made of six sheets of corrugated iron bolted at the top with steel plates at each end, they measured six feet, six inches by four feet, six inches. At the entrance were a steel shield and an earthen blast wall. They were built to house up to six people. Wealthy families paid for their own; the cost was £7. The government provided the Anderson Shelters for lower-income families who earned less than £5 per week. By the time production had ended, 3.6 million had been manufactured.

Dampness was a problem with the Anderson Shelters, but as the air raids during the Blitz became a nightly event, people sometimes stayed in them rather than going back and forth to their homes every time the air raid sirens went off. The structures did not keep out the noise made by the bombs, and sleep was difficult, if not impossible, inside the shelter.

The Morrison Shelter, which was designed like a cage, was intended to provide shelter for people who did not have cellars or gardens and first appeared in March 1941. The family could use the Morrison Shelter inside their homes. They would assemble the 359 parts which made up the shelter, which measured six feet, six inches long, four feet wide, and two feet, six inches high. By the end of 1941, half a million Morrison Shelters had been distributed. The Morrison Shelter, named for Herbert Morrison, the Minister for Home Security, was made of heavy steel and could do double duty as a table.

London was a busy city, and not everyone would be at home close to their Morrison or Anderson Shelter when an air raid began. In March 1940, surface street communal shelters began to be built in order to accommodate the people who would be outside or in a public space at the onset of a raid. The shelters were designed so that they could hold 50 people, but because they were built in haste, the public was uncertain about their ability to protect from bombing.

The government was dubious at the prospect of using the underground system tunnels and stations for air raid shelters, but the people of London felt that they were safer underground than above it. The stations were supplied with first aid facilities, chemical toilets, and bunks. There were 124 canteens. Shelter marshals were assigned to provide first aid and assistance if the tunnels flooded. The underground began to be used as a shelter on September 21, 1940. On its busiest night, it sheltered 177,000 people who brought pillows, blankets, sandwiches, and thermoses with them to ride out the bombing attack.

When the Germans began their campaign of regular nightly bombing, it was not uncommon for Londoners to spend every night in a shelter of some kind. City living took on a new aspect; merely trying to get a night's sleep became a challenge. Sometimes, as the Germans were returning from a raid, they would drop bombs at random, rather than upon targets, in order to fly home in more safety. Some of the bombs fell around the cities and in the countryside in Kent which, because it was on the flight path to London, was given the name of Bomb Alley.

The Blitz was a time of great travail for the British public. But it was also a period of national unity, as the civilians worked together, confident of their purpose and cohesive in their resistance to the common enemy. During the eight months of the Blitz, the Luftwaffe dropped 50,000 tons of bombs in its attack upon the British civilians. Over a million people were left homeless, and more than 40,000 were killed. This was the first time in Europe that a civilian population was punished by bombing on such a massive scale.

Chapter Five

The London Blitz

"London was ripped and stabbed with fire."

—Ernie Pyle

Hitler had put the invasion of Great Britain on hold for the time being as, in September 1940, his Luftwaffe switched its tactics from targeting radar stations and RAF airfields to a direct effort to batter the morale of Londoners. By demoralizing the citizens, Hitler felt, he would force Great Britain to accept his terms.

On September 7, 1940, at 4:00 pm, 617 German fighters were escorted by 348 bombers. For two hours, they rained bombs on the city of London. Two hours after that, a second attack got underway; this one lasted until 4:30 the next morning. For the following 57 days, London would undergo fierce bombing during the period of the Battle of Britain that would come to be known as the Blitz. Much of the city was destroyed by fire from the bombs. During the night, over 170,000 people fled to the underground stations for shelter. A school that served as an air raid shelter became a grave as 450 people were killed when a bomb struck it; that was the most deadly single bombing incident during the Blitz.

But more was to come. September 15 would later come to be known as Battle of Britain Day, but for the people of Britain, it was the unleashing of Nazi terror from above. The Germans had unwittingly provided the RAF with a bit of a break by switching their methods to bombing London rather than attacking the RAF bases and radar stations. The RAF pilots had used the respite to repair and rest their planes as squadrons were replenished. The head of Fighter Command, Air-Chief Marshal Hugh Dowding, had brought planes to the southeast region of England from all over the country. The Germans, however, were convinced that the RAF was nearing the end of its ability to defend the nation. The day was to have two overwhelming bombing raids on London along with attacks on Southampton and Portland.

At 11:00 am on September 15, the first wave came into sight; 250 bombers crossing the Channel. The RAF intercepted half of the planes, but the rest went to London. At 2:00 pm, the second round appeared, heading for South London and the railways to Kent. The raiding went on through the night.

Prime Minister Churchill, who was visiting the headquarters of No. 11 Group, Fighter Command, which was responsible for the defense of southeast England and London, wrote, "Presently the red bulbs showed that the majority of our squadrons were engaged. In a little while, all our squadrons were fighting and some had already begun to return for fuel. All were in the air. The lower line of bulbs was out. There was not one squadron left in reserve".

Targeting London for raids, while it increased the distress for the civilians, also posed problems for the German aircraft. Their escort planes, with limited fuel capacity, only had ten minutes of flying time left by the time they reached their destination, after which they had to turn back home. That left the bombers undefended by fighter escorts. Germans adapted the Messerschmitts to improve this deficiency, but not until later in the autumn of 1940.

The RAF was able to scatter the bombers in their formations so that when the remaining bombers dropped their bombs, they weren't as deadly because they fell over a wider area. The raiding went on into the night, and during the day, thousands of civilians stared up at the sky to watch the aerial battle above.

The RAF shot down 61 planes, the highest losses to the Luftwaffe in more than a month, while the RAF lost 31 planes. It was a terrible ordeal to endure, but it did have one positive result. The Germans abandoned their daytime bombing of London, although the Blitz had not ended.

The Royal Family did not abandon London, staying in Buckingham Palace when they were not at Windsor Castle visiting princesses Elizabeth and Margaret. During the intense bombing of September 1940, Buckingham Palace was damaged. Bombs landed on the grounds and exploded just 80 yards away from where King George VI and Queen Elizabeth were located in a small sitting room. Elizabeth, mother of Queen Elizabeth II, had already explained the family's position when others urged the

Royal Family to escape to Canada for their safety. She assured the people that she and the children would not leave unless the king left, and that wasn't going to happen. "The King will not leave the country in any circumstances whatever."

But the night time bombing continued to do its utmost to bring destruction to the resisting Londoners. Famed World War II reporter Ernie Pyle wrote evocatively of a nighttime bombing during the Christmas season as 1940 came to an end. He recalled how, as the German planes flew overhead, he could feel his hotel room shaking from the vibration of the guns. He and some friends went to a darkened balcony that offered a generous view of the city. He wrote, "You have all seen big fires, but I doubt if you have ever seen the whole horizon of a city lined with great fires, scores of them, perhaps hundreds."

The sound of the bombs told him that buildings were being torn apart by the explosions. Fires were close enough that he could hear the flames as they crackled and he could hear the firemen yelling. Every two minutes, a fresh wave of planes flew over. Their motors, Pyle wrote, sounded like a bee buzzing in fury. At one point, he and his friends watched as two dozen incendiary bombs fell and went off within two seconds. The firefighters would hurry to smother them with sand to put out the flames, but too soon, another bomb would catch fire in another building. Directly in front of their balcony, they saw flames extending hundreds of feet into the air as smoke formed a great cloud overhead. They watched in disbelief as the dome of St. Paul's Cathedral emerged through the cloud. Fire surrounded the famed cathedral, and then the cathedral came slowly but clearly into view, like, Pyle wrote, "some miraculous figure that appears before peace-hungry soldiers on a battlefield."

Some time later, Pyle donned a tin hat and went out as the fires continued to burn. He found the scene riveting. "The thing I shall always remember above all the other things in my life is the monstrous loveliness of that one single view of London on a holiday night; London stabbed with great fires, shaken by explosions, its dark regions along the Thames sparkling with the pin points of white-hot bombs, all of it roofed over with a ceiling of pink that held bursting shells, balloons, flares and the grind of vicious engines. And in yourself the excitement and anticipation and wonder in your soul that this could be happening at all. These things all went together to make the most hateful, most beautiful single scene I have ever known."

Chapter Six

Churchill at War

"He took the English language and sent it into battle."

—Beverley Nichols

Neville Chamberlain's leadership at the onset of German aggression and the outbreak of war had not inspired the British government, and on May 10, 1940, as many members of the Labor Party refused to serve under him, Winston Churchill became prime minister. He had served in various government positions, and he had superb leadership skills and was an adept tactician. All of these abilities would come into play as he served the British people as their prime minister during one of the most challenging periods of their nation's history.

Churchill possessed a resume which thrived upon the diversity of his experience. Born to Lord Randolph Churchill and his American wife, Jennie Jerome, Churchill belonged to the privileged class; the first Duke of Marlborough, a military hero during the Stuart reign on the throne of England, was his ancestor. While serving in the British army, Churchill saw action in India and Sudan. He combined his military career with his writing skills, authoring military reports for newspapers and two books based on his experiences. He left the military in

1899 to work as a war correspondent. It was then that Churchill was taken prisoner while covering the Boer War in South Africa but managed to escape and later wrote a book about his dramatic exploits.

After winning a seat in Parliament in 1900, he continued his climb up the political ladder. As First Lord of the Admiralty, he promoted the modernization of the Royal Navy and, foreseeing the potential of flight for military use, set up the Royal Navy Air Service. After the disaster at the Battle of Gallipoli during World War I, Churchill left the government in 1915 and rejoined the British Army, serving on the Western Front. In 1917, back in the government, he oversaw the production of munitions, tanks, and airplanes in his role as minister of munitions.

In 1929, seemingly out of touch with political mainstream thinking, Churchill left the government and began to concentrate his efforts on his writing, publishing a biography of his celebrated ancestor, the first Duke of Marlborough and also beginning his work on *A History of the English-Speaking Peoples*. In 1953, he would be awarded the Nobel Prize for Literature; the citation would read "for his mastery of historical and biographical description as well as for brilliant oratory in defending exalted human values."

Exalting human values was part of what motivated Churchill's efforts as prime minister; he regarded the Nazis as particularly evil and lacking in those values which he held dear. During the 1930s, as Adolf Hitler drove Germany forward in a program of aggressive military expansion, Churchill began to recognize the threat that Nazism posed to Europe, and by the late 1930s, he was a forceful proponent of British rearmament. At the onset of World War II, he was Great Britain's First Lord of the Admiralty and part of the government's war cabinet. He had vehemently proposed that Great Britain should be proactive against Germany by occupying the iron mines and sea ports of Norway, but Chamberlain resisted his arguments.

On May 10, Chamberlain resigned as prime minister, and Churchill replaced him, the same day that the Nazis were advancing toward the Low Countries. Churchill's coalition cabinet included members from the Labor, Conservative, and Liberal parties, a show of unity that reflected the need for a united government and country against a fearful enemy. On June 18, Churchill spoke to the House of Commons. The Battle of Britain, he told them, was about to start.

Military experts might have thought that words were a paltry defense against a foe like Adolf Hitler, but Winston Churchill understood that if the British people were to be able to withstand the terrible onslaught which the Nazis intended to throw at them, they needed to be confident in their leaders. Churchill's stirring words did what bullets could not have done: they fortified the British people with an invincible conviction that they were engaged in a cosmic battle against an enemy which sought to extinguish all that was noble and progressive in civilization.

It was his oratory that rallied the English people during this era, and his indomitable courage that inspired his people as the Germans poured bombs upon them. In his first speech as prime minister, his aim was to calm the fears of the nation but also to instruct the government in which all parties, regardless of their political slant, would unite to fight the Germans. He was eloquent and confident: he could offer the people, he said, nothing except "blood, toil, tears, and sweat." The aim? "Victory."

After the evacuation of the British troops from Dunkirk, Churchill warned of the struggle that lay ahead. He did not minimize the dangers that awaited, but even in his stark forecast of the future, his eloquence was like a shot of adrenaline to his listeners. "We shall defend our Island, whatever the cost may be; we shall fight on the beaches, we shall fight on the landing grounds, we shall fight in the fields and in the streets, we shall fight in the hills; we shall never surrender."

Not long after that, more bad news awaited the Allies, as France fell to the Germans. In that speech on June 18, 1940, Churchill reminded his people that although they were alone in the fight, the fight was vital if civilization was to be preserved. "But if we fail, then the whole world, including the United States, including all that we have known and cared for, will sink into the abyss of a new Dark Age made more sinister, and perhaps more protracted, by the lights of perverted science. Let us therefore brace ourselves to our duties, and so bear ourselves that, if the British Empire and its

Commonwealth last for a thousand years, men will still say, 'This was their finest hour.'"

By the end of 1941, the United States had joined the Allies following the Japanese attack on Pearl Harbor on December 7. Addressing the joint houses of Congress on December 26, Churchill reminded his American audience of his own Anglo-American pedigree. He was able to expand upon the shared heritage of Great Britain and the United States, predicting that as allies fighting together for the common good, they would prevail: "In the days to come the British and American peoples will for their own safety and for the good of all walk together side by side in majesty, in justice and in peace." He also injected humor into the grim circumstances with his comment that "if my father had been American and my mother British, instead of the other way round, I might have got here on my own."

Although the United States had suffered from the attack in the Pacific, Churchill persuaded the Americans to help Britain by focusing on the European war against the Germans rather than restricting their efforts to the Pacific. He and President Franklin Roosevelt enjoyed a robust partnership as they steered their countries toward victory and peace and the roots of the "special relationship" between Great Britain and the United States were firmly planted.

Churchill would live to be 90 years old, and he would again serve his country as prime minister in the 1950s. But it is his service as the prime minister during World War II that would define his destiny, and the British people would not forget him. In 2002, in a survey to name the greatest Briton of all time, Winston Churchill received 447,423 votes and won the honor.

Conclusion

The End of the Battle of Britain

"Directive 21: The German Wehrmacht must be prepared to crush Soviet Russia in a quick campaign (Operation Barbarossa) even before the conclusion of the war against England."

—Adolf Hitler

The massive raids on September 15 failed in their goal of bringing England to its knees, forcing the Germans to re-evaluate their timeline for the invasion. With its loss of 1,636 aircraft, the Luftwaffe was running out of both planes and crew. The Germans had failed to realize the scale of production of aircraft by the British, and they also underestimated the size of the Royal Air Force. On the other hand, the British overestimated the number of German planes and the capacity of its aircraft manufacturing production. The Germans were convinced that the RAF was nearing the end of its ability to defend Great Britain, while the RAF believed that the enemy had an ever greater number of planes and pilots waiting to fly.

Hitler, in a meeting at his headquarters on September 14, realized that the Luftwaffe, despite Goering's confidence, had failed to establish its supremacy of the air. By September 17, he said, he would consider settling on a date for invading Great Britain; either September 27 or October 8, he estimated. But by that time, after the Luftwaffe had pounded London with its September 15 attack and Great Britain was still obstinately refusing to be cowed, Hitler realized that the RAF was not on the brink of surrender. Operation Sea Lion would have to be postponed for the time being.

The Luftwaffe could not afford to continue losing men or planes at its current rate; during the raiding on August 18, the Luftwaffe lost five trained crew members who were killed, captured, or wounded, for every RAF pilot who was killed or wounded. British civilian losses, however, were heavy. From July to December 1940, more than 23,000 British civilians were killed and more than 32,000 wounded.

The Battle of Britain had been a costly one, but there were positive results for the British as the encounter dealt the Germany military its first major defeat. The RAF had successfully defended Great Britain against German aerial attack and had, by doing so, discouraged Hitler's plans to invade. British military officers felt that it was the Luftwaffe, dismayed at the number of planes and men it was using, that caved, losing morale as the RAF gained.

The British people, who had had their confidence buoyed by their success in evacuating their army at Dunkirk, were fortified by the knowledge that they had come through the London Blitz without capitulating. They were bloody but unbowed. Watching from across the Atlantic, the Americans, as yet still neutral, were impressed. But President Franklin Roosevelt, knowing that eventually his country would be drawn into the global battle, wanted more information than what he had gotten from American Ambassador Joseph Kennedy, who believed that Great Britain could not survive the bombing. His messenger returned with the perspective that not only would the British withstand the German raids, but that the United States should offer its support.

September 15 would be remembered as Battle of Britain Day, the date when the entire RAF was engaged in the defense of London and the country's southeast region, ultimately proving to be the turning point in the Battle of Britain.

By the spring of 1941, Hitler was deep in preparations for the invasion of the Soviet Union. His determination to conquer the giant land mass of Russia would be a devastating defeat. There were many battles still to be fought in the global conflict, and Churchill recognized that the battle was not yet won when he said in the House of Commons on November 1942, "Now this is not the end. It is not even the beginning of the end. But it is, perhaps, the end of the beginning." The words came as the Allies drove the Germans out of Egypt at the Battle of Alamein. The tide of battle would turn in the Allies' favor. They would invade Normandy in June 1944 and march to Germany. Germany would lose the war; the Allies would win.

But Great Britain would lose, too. The empire upon which the sun never set would see its colonies seek their independence after the war. India would, under the leadership of Gandhi, fight for its freedom to be its own nation. Throughout the 1950s and 1960s, countries in the Middle East, Asia, Africa, and the Caribbean would lower the British Union Jack and fly their own flags. But there was a crucial difference. Those nations did not fall under the control of Nazi Germany. Although they were lost to England, they became free nations, not occupied territories subject to Nazi authority. The loss of empire was one of the by-products of the Second World War, one not envisioned by the imperial British.

But when the war was over and the soldiers returned home, there was more than victory to be celebrated. The British had outlasted the might of the German military. The British people who had rescued their army with their civilian armada of "little ships" at Dunkirk had continued to show their fortitude throughout the Battle of Britain, when the Luftwaffe stormed the skies and threw everything it had at the British people and, in the end, was forced to admit defeat.

The fall into the abyss of a new Dark Age that Churchill had warned of should Nazi Germany triumph did not happen. The modern world continues to host violence, bloodshed, genocide, oppression, and the other terrors that emerge from the Pandora's box of geopolitical strife. But the Allied victory over Adolf Hitler's Germany ushered in a Europe which has seen far less bloodshed and turmoil than it had in the centuries prior to 1945. The Battle of Britain, and the resolution of the British people and their prime minister, stand as evidence that ultimately democracy is a battle fought and won not only by brave pilots and stalwart soldiers and sailors but also by determined civilians.

Made in the USA
Columbia, SC
07 February 2021

32453865R00026